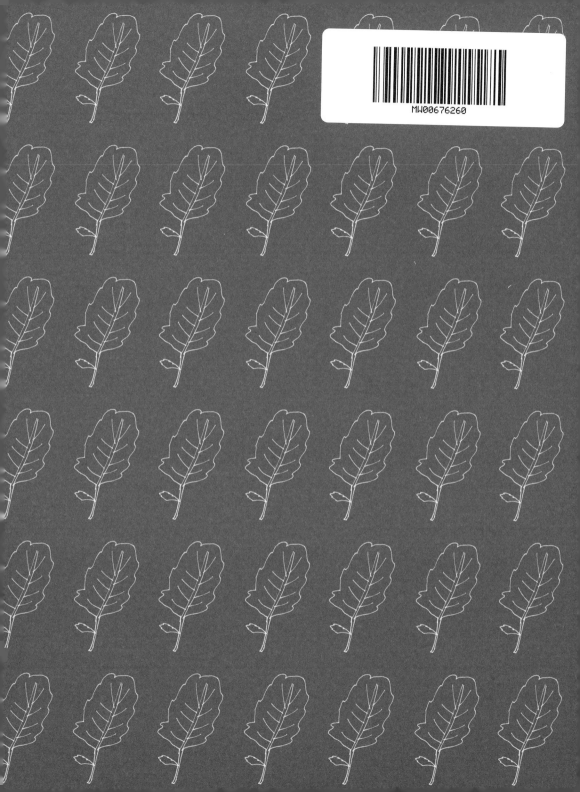

GREENS

THE GOODNESS OF

GREENS

40 INCREDIBLE NUTRIENT-PACKED RECIPES

EDITED BY **CLAIRE ROGERS**
KYLE BOOKS

CONTENTS

GREENS ARE GREAT

From dark, leafy, iron-filled kale to bright, crisp beans, and springy, vitamin-rich watercress, there are so many ways to enjoy eating your greens. Once relegated to the side of the meal, here they take center stage and are celebrated for their delicious, nutritious goodness.

Whether you're a dedicated veg-eater or just want to up your intake, you will find plenty of recipes to whet your appetite in the following pages, divided into chapters arranged by type: Beans & Legumes (peas, snow peas, green beans, fava beans); Leafy Greens (spinach, watercress, chard, lettuce, arugula); and Brassicas (kale, cabbage, broccoli, Brussels sprouts).

You'll find recipes for all these green veggies and interesting ways to prepare them. Cabbage leaves used as wraps, raw Brussels sprouts in salad, a gorgeous green salad incorporating no less than four different greens, plus soups, salads, juices, stir-fries, and, yes, even kale chips (see page 67)! There is so much to choose from.

THE GOODNESS OF GREENS

Greens, particularly dark leafy ones such as kale and spinach, are packed full of vitamins and minerals that help maintain both a healthy appearance (skin and hair) and healthy insides (your bones and your gut among others). Studies have suggested that vegetables rich in antioxidants and phytonutrients, such as cruciferous vegetables (broccoli, cabbage, etc.) and dark leafy greens are linked to a reduced risk of heart disease and even some cancers.

Fresh is best

Vegetables lose nutrients from the moment they are picked, so the fresher the better. It can be several days from when they are picked to when they are stocked on supermarket shelves. Frozen vegetables are a good alternative if you can't find fresh. These are generally frozen very soon after they are picked, which helps preserve the nutrients. Some supermarkets also stock "living salads" that can be placed on a windowsill and harvested as needed.

BUYING THE BEST

In order to get the most vitamins and minerals from your greens, you need to buy the freshest produce possible. Farmers' markets are excellent sources of organic, pesticide-free vegetables, but you can also grow your own.

Top tips for buying good greens

♦ Always buy as fresh as possible.
♦ Avoid anything with wilting leaves or leaves starting to turn yellow.
♦ Choose greens with the brightest, crispest colors.
♦ Check stalks—you want them to be firm, not bendy.

STORING

Most green vegetables are best stored in the refrigerator to keep them fresh for longer. Some will last longer than others; beans and greens with tightly-packed leaves (broccoli, Brussels sprouts, cabbage) usually last up to a week; soft, looser-leaved greens (kale, Swiss chard, watercress) will only last about 3 days. If you store your greens in plastic bags, make sure there are holes to allow airflow. There is no need to wash broccoli, peas and lettuce before storing in the fridge; simply wash when you are ready to use them.

BEANS & LEGUMES

SPRING PEA SOUP

*GLUTEN-FREE

Use fresh peas for this soup, as they have enough body to yield a creamier texture. Better yet are petits pois—spring peas harvested very young and tender. Serve this hot or chilled to suit the weather outside.

Serves 4

1½ pounds fresh peas, shelled (reserve pea pods)
1 medium onion, diced
3 cloves garlic, chopped
1 medium potato, peeled and diced
1 quart gluten-free vegetable stock
8 ice cubes
¼ cup crème fraîche
Sea salt
Lemon juice to taste

To serve
⅓ cup mint leaves, julienned
12 pea flowers
6 pea shoots
1 tablespoon lemon zest, finely julienned

1. In a medium saucepan over high heat, blanch the shelled peas in boiling salted water until their color brightens, or 20 to 30 seconds. Drain the peas and immediately plunge them into a bowl of iced water. After the peas have chilled, drain and set aside.

2. In a medium saucepan over medium-high heat, combine the reserved pea pods, onion, garlic, potato, and stock. Boil until the stock is reduced to three-quarters of its original volume and the potato is very tender, or about 40 minutes.

3. Transfer to a blender or food processor. Add half of the reserved peas. Blend until velvety smooth, adding water if the soup is too thick to easily puree. Pass through a fine strainer. Add the ice cubes and crème fraîche and stir until the ice cubes have melted. Season with salt and lemon juice and place in the fridge to fully chill, about 1 hour. To serve the soup warm, return it to the saucepan and warm fully over low heat, for 10 to 15 minutes.

4. Divide the soup into four soup bowls. Top each with the mint leaves, pea flowers and shoots, and lemon zest. Serve immediately.

When making chilled soup, add ice cubes at the end to cool the soup quickly and thin it out. It helps to keep the color of green vegetable soups brighter.

PEA, MINT & PINE NUT SOUP *DAIRY-FREE

Pine nuts give the soup a luxuriously creamy texture and the mint makes it taste like a bowlful of spring.

Serves 1

1 cup frozen or fresh peas
1 garlic clove, peeled
¾ cup chicken stock or water
2 tablespoons pine nuts, toasted
1 tablespoon olive oil
A handful of fresh mint leaves
Sea salt and freshly ground black pepper

1. Place the peas, garlic, and stock in a saucepan. Bring to a boil. Turn off the heat and let it sit for 3 minutes.

2. Grind the pine nuts to a paste in a blender or with a mortar and pestle. Trickle in the olive oil and give it a good mix.

3. Place the peas in a blender with the pine nut paste and fresh mint. Pulse to a smooth puree. Add more stock if needed. If you want a smoother soup, pass it through a strainer. Season to taste and serve.

BEET, PEA & WATERCRESS

GLUTEN-FREE

This salad has so many flavors and textures going on that the added slivers of roast lamb are like the icing on top.

Serves 4

2 to 3 tablespoons of olive oil, plus more for drizzling
2 beets, cut into ¾-inch wedges
A drizzle of honey
2 cups frozen peas
3 cups watercress
Salt and freshly ground black pepper
Juice and zest of ½ lemon
Boiled new potatoes
4½ ounces cold roast lamb, chopped

For the dressing
⅓ cup plain or Greek yogurt
1 garlic clove, finely minced
¼ cup grated cucumber
A few fresh mint leaves

1. Splash some olive oil into a large frying pan. Add the beets and sauté until tender, 10 to 15 minutes. Drizzle with the honey. Set aside to cool.

2. Place the peas in a colander and rinse in warm water until they are defrosted.

3. Divide the watercress between the plates. Season with salt and pepper, drizzle with the lemon juice and olive oil, scatter with the lemon zest, and toss to combine. Arrange the beets among the watercress, then add the potatoes. Sprinkle in the peas and gently mix through the watercress leaves. Dot the lamb over the top.

4. For the dressing, mix the yogurt with the garlic, cucumber, and mint, and season to taste. Drizzle this over the top of the salad and serve.

GREEN PEA RAVIOLI

Fresh peas are obviously a lot more work for the preparation of these ravioli, but really do make a difference.

Serves 6 to 8

For the pasta dough
2 cups bread flour
2 large eggs, beaten
1 large egg yolk, beaten
1 tablespoon olive oil

For the green pea ravioli
2 cups shelled peas (or frozen)
⅔ cup mint leaves
½ cup good-quality ricotta
  cheese, well drained
2 scallions, finely chopped
Salt and freshly
  ground black pepper
1 tablespoon lemon juice

For the saffron butter sauce
⅔ cup good vegetable stock
½ cup heavy cream
Good pinch of quality saffron
  (or ½ teaspoon powdered)
3 tablespoons unsalted butter,
  chilled and cut into pieces

For the truffled beet salad
1 tablespoon balsamic vinegar
Pinch of sugar
½ tablespoon truffle oil
1 medium beet, cooked, peeled,
  and very thinly sliced
1 truffle, very thinly sliced
  (optional)
¾ cup pea shoots

1. Blend all the pasta ingredients and 1 tablespoon of water in a food processor for a few seconds to mix—do not overwork the dough. Remove, then knead the dough until soft and pliable. Wrap in plastic wrap and put in the fridge for 1 hour to rest.

2. Cook the peas in just enough boiling water to cover for 5 to 6 minutes until tender and then drain, reserving ½ cup of the cooking water. Refresh in iced water, drain, and dry them well. Place in a food processor with the mint, ricotta, and scallions and blend to a coarse puree. Transfer to a bowl, season to taste, and add the lemon juice.

3. Roll out the pasta into thin sheets, then brush a sheet with water and place tablespoons of the pea-ricotta mixture on it, about 2 inches apart in rows. Cover with a second sheet of pasta, press down gently around the fillings, then cut the pasta into squares. Check to ensure the edges are well sealed, place on a lightly floured pan, and let dry for 20 minutes.

4. For the saffron butter, heat the vegetable stock, reserved pea cooking liquid, cream, and saffron in a pan and simmer until the liquid has reduced by half. Remove from the heat, whisk in the chilled butter, season to taste, and then finely strain.

5. Cook the ravioli in plenty of simmering water for 3 to 4 minutes until *al dente*, then remove with a slotted spoon and drain well.

6. For the salad, whisk together the vinegar, sugar, and oil, add the beets and truffle, and adjust the seasoning; mix well.

7. Divide the ravioli between four serving dishes, pour over the saffron sauce, top with the beet salad and pea shoots, and serve immediately.

ASIAN CRAWFISH WITH SNOW PEAS

*DAIRY-FREE

Crawfish is considered a huge pest in many waters, as it tends to eat native river life. It seems only right that we do our bit to control this pest by encouraging you to put it on your plate!

Serves 6

For the salad

1 cup black rice
2 cups snow peas
2½ cups dried egg noodles
1¾ pounds crawfish tails, cooked and peeled
½ Chinese cabbage, shredded
1 red bell pepper, seeded and diced into ½-inch cubes
2 scallions, finely chopped
1 cup sliced almonds, toasted
2 carrots, cut into ribbons with a ribbon peeler
1 cucumber, cut into ribbons with a ribbon peeler

For the dressing

1 tablespoon finely chopped fresh cilantro
3 tablespoons rice wine vinegar
2 tablespoons soy sauce
Juice of 1 lime
2-inch piece of fresh ginger, peeled and grated
1 teaspoon sugar
1 tablespoon olive oil

1. Preheat the oven to 350°F.

2. Place the rice in a medium pan of boiling water and cook for 15 minutes or until soft and cooked. Drain and rinse under cold water. Set aside. Meanwhile, blanch the snow peas in a pan of boiling salted water for 4 minutes, then drain and rinse under cold water.

3. Place the noodles on a baking sheet and bake until golden brown. Let cool and then crush them with your hands.

4. Combine all the dressing ingredients in a small glass pitcher or bowl and whisk until thoroughly mixed. Place all the salad ingredients in a large serving bowl and stir to combine. Add the dressing... badabing!

SNOW PEA & ARTICHOKE SALAD

*DAIRY-FREE

There is nothing to beat this crisp, fruity salad. Serve it as a dinner-party knockout or just a lazy weekend treat.

Serves 4 as a side

½ pound baby artichokes
⅓ pound Jerusalem artichokes
2½ cups snow peas

For the dressing
Zest of ½ orange, cut into long shreds
Juice of ½ orange
1 teaspoon whole-grain mustard
1½ tablespoons champagne vinegar
2½ tablespoons virgin olive oil
¼ cup walnut oil
Salt and freshly ground black pepper

1. Prepare the baby artichokes by removing the stalks and trimming ½-inch off the tops of the leaves. As they are very young and tender, no other preparation is required.

2. Peel the Jerusalem artichokes. Cook the baby and Jerusalem artichokes in separate pans of boiling salted water for 8 to 10 minutes or until tender, then drain. Blanch the snow peas in boiling water for 2 minutes. Drain and refresh under cold water, then drain again.

3. For the dressing, blanch the orange zest in boiling water for 1 minute, then refresh under cold water and drain well. Whisk together all the dressing ingredients, adding seasoning to taste.

4. Place the artichokes in a bowl, pour over the dressing, then add the snow peas. Serve at room temperature.

THAI GREEN VEGETABLE CURRY

*VEGETARIAN *DAIRY-FREE

The addition of sweet pineapple to this vibrant curry gives it a real lift. The green chile adds a little extra heat but this can be left out if you prefer a more subtly spiced dish.

Serves 6

1 tablespoon vegetable oil
2 large shallots, chopped
1 green chile, seeded
   and finely chopped
3 tablespoons Thai green
   curry paste
½ cup red lentils
2 leeks, washed and sliced
1 red and 1 yellow bell pepper,
   seeded and thickly sliced
2 cups butternut squash,
   peeled and cubed
1 cup green beans, trimmed
   and cut into 1-inch lengths
1¼ cups light coconut milk
1 (8-ounce) can pineapple
   rings, drained and cut
   into chunks
5½ ounces spinach leaves
Sea salt and freshly
   ground black pepper

To garnish
A large handful of fresh
   cilantro, chopped
⅔ cup cashews, toasted
   in a dry pan

1. Heat the vegetable oil in a large, nonstick pan over low-medium heat. Add the shallots and green chile and cook gently for a few minutes. Add the curry paste and cook gently for another 2 minutes, stirring frequently.

2. Stir the lentils into the paste then add the leeks, bell peppers, squash, beans, and coconut milk. Bring to a boil, then lower the heat and simmer, covered, for about 20 minutes, by which time the lentils should be very soft.

3. Stir in the pineapple pieces and add the spinach leaves. Cover the pan and simmer for 2 more minutes, by which time the spinach will have wilted and can be stirred easily into the sauce.

4. Taste and adjust the seasoning. Serve with Thai jasmine rice and top with fresh cilantro and toasted cashews.

Sweet potato or
even pumpkin can
be used in place of
butternut squash.

RED TOFU & FRENCH
BEANS *VEGETARIAN *DAIRY-FREE

This delicate marinade adds a sweet yet hot coating to the tofu, topping a wonderfully fragrant and fresh salad.

Serves 4

9-ounce package firm tofu,
  drained
1 tablespoon honey
2 tablespoons plum sauce
2 tablespoons soy sauce
3 teaspoons sweet chili sauce
12 ounces French beans,
  ends trimmed
2 tablespoons cashews,
  roasted and chopped
2 persimmons, stem removed
  and cut into wedges
Salt and freshly ground
  black pepper
2 tablespoons peanut
  or vegetable oil

For the dressing
2 tablespoons palm
  or brown sugar
2 tablespoons coarse sea salt
2 garlic cloves, chopped
A good handful of mint leaves
4 hot green chiles,
  seeded and chopped
½-inch piece of fresh ginger,
  peeled and grated
3 tablespoons vegetarian fish
  sauce (*nuoc mam chay*)
Juice of 8 limes
4 shallots, thinly sliced

1. Cut the tofu in half widthwise, then cut both pieces in half horizontally to give four equally thick slices. In a shallow dish combine the honey with the plum, soy, and sweet chili sauces. Place the tofu slices in the marinade and let marinate for 2 hours, turning regularly to ensure the tofu is thoroughly coated.

2. For the dressing, melt the sugar in a small pan. Place the salt, garlic, and mint in a mortar and lightly pound to a pulp with a pestle. Add the chiles, palm sugar, and ginger and pound again. Add the fish sauce, lime juice, and shallots and mix well. Leave for 1 hour for the flavors to develop.

3. Cook the beans in a pan of boiling salted water for 2 to 3 minutes or until just cooked, but still retaining a good bite.

4. Place the beans, cashews, and persimmons in a bowl and pour over the prepared dressing. Toss well and season to taste. Remove the tofu from the marinade. Heat a large frying pan with the oil, add the tofu, and cook for about 2 minutes on each side until golden and crisp. Place a good pile of the salad on four serving plates, top each with a slice of tofu, and serve at once.

GREEN BEANS & LAMB BROCHETTES
*GLUTEN-FREE

A lemony yogurt dressing forms the base of this salad. If you cut the green beans in half lengthwise, this is attractive and makes for a more delicate bite. But this isn't a must, and can be skipped if you prefer not to fuss.

Serves 4

1¼ pounds boneless leg of lamb or lamb shoulder, cut into 1-inch cubes

2 garlic cloves, very thinly sliced

¾ teaspoon piment d'Espelette or ¼ teaspoon cayenne pepper

½ pound green beans, trimmed and halved lengthwise

½ pound sugar snap peas, strings removed

2 small red onions, cut into ½-inch wedges, root end intact

5 tablespoons extra virgin olive oil

A handful plus 1 tablespoon coarsely chopped mint

For the dressing
Zest and juice of 1 lemon
⅓ cup Greek yogurt
Sea salt and freshly ground black pepper

Metal skewers, or wooden skewers soaked in water for 10 minutes

1. Place the lamb, lemon zest, garlic, and piment d'Espelette into a bowl, then cover and marinate at room temperature for 1 hour or in the fridge overnight. If marinating the meat overnight, bring it to room temperature before broiling.

2. Bring a medium saucepan of salted water to a boil. Add the beans and peas and cook for about 1½ minutes just until crisp-tender. Drain, place in a large bowl, and set aside.

3. For the dressing, squeeze 2 tablespoons of lemon juice into a bowl, then add the yogurt and a generous pinch of salt and pepper, stir together, and set aside.

4. Preheat the broiler to medium-high.

5. Toss the onions with 1½ tablespoons of oil and season generously. Broil, turning occasionally, until golden and tender, about 5 minutes. Transfer to a plate to cool slightly.

6. Toss the lamb with 1 tablespoon of oil and season generously. Thread the lamb pieces onto the skewers and broil for 3 to 4 minutes, turning occasionally, until cooked to medium-rare. Transfer to a cutting board and let rest for 5 minutes.

7. Meanwhile, add the onion wedges, mint, remaining oil, and a generous pinch each of salt and pepper to the bowl with the green bean mixture. Gently toss together, then taste and adjust the seasoning.

8. Spoon the yogurt mixture onto four serving plates and top with the bean salad and skewers.

SPRING SALAD WITH GOAT CHEESE *VEGETARIAN

Use this dressing for all kinds of salads—tomatoes and basil, grilled zucchini and eggplant, sliced avocados, or a simple leaf salad. Gremolata is a classic garnish for osso bucco, but you can also scatter it over grilled meats, vegetables, or fish for an instant lift. Try to buy peas and fava beans still in the pod rather than in prepared packs—they'll be fresher and more flavorful.

Serves 4 as an appetizer or light lunch

A large bunch of asparagus
1½ cups shelled peas
1½ cups shelled fava beans
3 ounces baby leaf spinach
A handful of pea shoots
4 slices of sourdough bread
7-ounce ash-covered young
   goat cheese log

For the gremolata
2 garlic cloves, finely chopped
¼ cup finely chopped
   flat-leaf parsley
Fine strips of zest from
   an organic lemon
2 tablespoons chopped
   pitted green olives
Sea salt flakes and freshly
   ground black pepper

For the lemon dressing
Juice of 1 lemon
¼ cup extra virgin olive oil
1 teaspoon Dijon mustard
1 teaspoon honey

1. Trim the tough ends of the asparagus and cut into 2-inch lengths. Bring a saucepan of salted water to a boil and blanch the asparagus for 3 minutes or until tender, then refresh in a bowl of iced water. Blanch the peas in the same pan for 1 to 2 minutes and add to the asparagus. Cook the fava beans in the same water for 1 to 2 minutes and then drain. Rinse under cold water and then slide each bean from its outer jacket to reveal the bright green, tender bean inside. Drain all the veggies and pat dry on paper towels.

2. To make the gremolata, combine all the ingredients in a small bowl and season.

3. Next make the dressing: Squeeze the juice from the lemon into a bowl, add the olive oil and mustard, and whisk to combine. Taste and add the honey, then season.

4. Toss the beans, peas, and asparagus in the dressing and arrange on plates with the baby leaf spinach and pea shoots.

5. Toast the sourdough on both sides under the broiler. Slice the goat cheese into ½-inch thick discs and place one slice on each piece of toast. Flash the cheese under the broiler again until it starts to soften. Spoon the gremolata alongside, drizzle with a little more oil, and serve immediately with the salad.

FAVA BEAN & BLUE CHEESE PIZZA *VEGETARIAN

This fennel sauce is also a delicious base for a seaweed pizza, or a kale, spinach, or broccoli pizza. It also freezes perfectly so make the full amount and use as needed.

Makes 1 pizza
(Dough makes 4 × 5½-ounce balls; can be frozen)

For the dough
1⅛ cups cold tap water
2½ teaspoons (½ ounce) fresh yeast
3¼ cups 00 flour, plus extra for dusting
½ tablespoon dairy salt

For the fennel sauce
1 tablespoon extra virgin olive oil
2 onions, thinly sliced
3 garlic cloves, crushed
5 bulbs of fennel, thinly sliced
Sea salt and freshly ground black pepper

For the pizza
20 fava beans
Semolina, for sprinkling
1 teaspoon extra virgin olive oil
A pinch of sea salt
8 cubes of blue cheese, approx. ½-inch
A large handful of grated mozzarella
1 teaspoon finely chopped flat-leaf parsley, to serve
Lemon wedges, to serve

1. First make the pizza dough: Put the water into the bowl of a food processor. Crumble the yeast into the flour and add to the water along with the salt. Mix for 5 minutes on medium speed. Let the dough rest for 5 minutes, then mix for another 20 minutes. The dough should be smooth and stick to the side of the mixing bowl.

2. Put the dough in an airtight container four times bigger than the dough. Refrigerate for at least 6 hours, preferably overnight.

3. Sprinkle a work surface with a little flour, then weigh and divide the dough into four 5½-ounce pieces using a small knife. Knead the dough into round balls roughly the size of tennis balls, transfer to a pan, sprinkle with flour, and refrigerate for 6 hours. Remove from the fridge 1 hour before you cook the pizza.

4. Meanwhile, make the fennel sauce: heat the oil in a pan, add the onions and garlic, and sweat until soft but not colored. Add the fennel slices and 2½ cups water, then season and simmer for 25 minutes or until soft. Blend until smooth. Taste and correct the seasoning, if necessary.

5. Preheat the oven to 475°F. Blanch the fava beans in boiling water for 2 minutes. Drain, refresh under cold running water, and set aside.

6. Roll the pizza dough into a 10-inch circle. Sprinkle a little semolina over a large baking sheet and put the pizza base on top. Drizzle the olive oil over the base of the pizza and sprinkle with the salt. Spread ⅔ cup of the fennel sauce over the base. Scatter over the fava beans and blue cheese and top with the mozzarella.

7. Bake in the oven for 10 to 12 minutes, or until the base is crisp and the top is bubbly and golden. Sprinkle with parsley and serve immediately, with lemon wedges.

FREEKEH & FAVA BEAN SALAD *VEGETARIAN *DAIRY-FREE

Earthy, slightly smoky, nutty, and nutrient-rich, freekeh (pronounced free-ka) is one of the most popular grains for salads and side dishes. Look for it in Middle Eastern food stores and online. If freekeh is unavailable, try barley or whole wheat pasta. Peas can be used in place of fava beans. Roasting lemons is one of the best techniques. The slightly charred slices hint at preserved lemons, although they are a little less intense.

Serves 4 to 6

1¾ cups freekeh
Fine sea salt and freshly ground black pepper
7 tablespoons extra virgin olive oil
1 pound asparagus, trimmed
1 lemon, rinsed and dried, end trimmed and cut crosswise into ⅛-inch thick rounds
1 large red onion, finely chopped
2 garlic cloves, thinly sliced
½ teaspoon fennel seeds, finely ground
1¾ cups shelled fresh fava beans (about 2¼ pounds in pods) or frozen fava beans, thawed
1 to 2 teaspoons Aleppo pepper or a pinch of cayenne pepper

1. Preheat the broiler. Line a rimmed baking sheet with parchment paper.

2. In a large saucepan, combine 4 cups of water, the freekeh, 1 teaspoon of salt, and 1 tablespoon of oil. Bring to a boil over high heat, then reduce to a gentle simmer, cover, and cook for 40 to 45 minutes, until the freekeh is tender but still has a bite and the water is mostly absorbed.

3. Meanwhile, broil the asparagus for 10 to 12 minutes, depending on thickness, until crisp-tender. Transfer to a plate and, while hot, drizzle with 1 tablespoon of oil and season generously.

4. Heat the oven to 375°F. Lay the lemon slices in a single layer on the prepared baking sheet, then drizzle with 2 tablespoons of

oil and season with ¼ teaspoon each of salt and black pepper.

5. Roast the lemon slices for 18 to 24 minutes until golden, rotating the pan halfway through and transferring any quick-browning slices to a plate as they're ready. (Keep a careful eye on the slices; you want a nice golden color.) Transfer the roasted slices to a plate to cool, then finely chop.

6. When the freekeh is ready, drain any excess water, then transfer to a large bowl.

7. Meanwhile, heat the remaining 3 tablespoons of oil in a large nonstick frying pan over medium-high heat. Add the onion, garlic, fennel seeds, and a generous pinch of salt. Reduce the heat to medium-low and gently cook for about

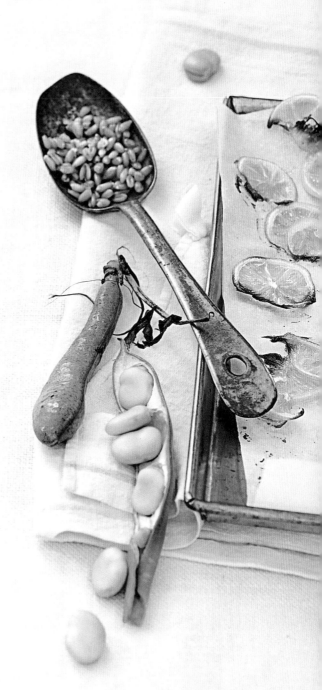

10 minutes, stirring occasionally, until the onion is tender. Add the chopped lemon and stir to combine. Cook for another 2 minutes, then remove the pan from the heat.

8. Meanwhile, cook the fava beans in salted boiling water for 2 minutes. Drain and run under cold water to cool, then peel if using fresh beans. Add the beans and the onion mixture to the bowl with the freekeh. Cut the asparagus into 1-inch lengths and add it as well.

9. Add ¼ teaspoon of salt and the Aleppo pepper or cayenne, then stir to combine. Adjust the seasoning to taste and serve.

LEAFY
GREENS

JUICY CHICKEN WITH & GARLIC SPINACH

*DAIRY-FREE

This slightly, or perhaps very, obscure way of cooking chicken breasts is based on the *recherché* restaurant technique of cooking *sous vide*. This is the rustic take on the method, which gives you an exceptionally tender and succulent interior without sacrificing the crisp outside.

Serves 4

2½ tablespoons extra
  virgin olive oil
18 ounces spinach, washed
  and dried
4 free-range chicken
  breasts, skin on
1½ quarts chicken or
  vegetable stock
Sea salt and freshly ground
  black pepper
3 garlic cloves, peeled
  and finely sliced
1 to 2 teaspoons finely
  sliced medium-hot
  red chile
Lemon wedges, to serve

1. Heat a tablespoon of oil in a large frying pan, add a pile of spinach leaves (you will need to cook them in batches), and toss until they wilt. Transfer to a bowl and proceed with the remainder.

2. Lay the chicken breasts skin-side down on a cutting board, flatten them with your hands, and cut out the white tendon from the underside if visible.

3. Bring the stock to a boil in a medium to large saucepan and season with salt. Turn the heat down as low as possible. Immerse the chicken breasts in the stock and cook for 15 minutes, without boiling. Transfer them to a plate and pat dry with paper towels. The stock can be used again: first pour it through a fine strainer, discarding any sediment in the bottom.

4. Heat ½ tablespoon of oil in a large frying pan over medium heat, season the chicken breasts well, and cook for several minutes on each side until golden. You may need to do this in batches, or use two pans.

5. Just before the chicken is ready, heat a tablespoon of oil in another frying pan over medium heat, add the garlic and chile, and cook briefly until fragrant and lightly colored, then stir in the spinach, season with salt, and heat through. Serve the chicken and spinach accompanied by lemon wedges.

SPINACH TART

Spinach is one of the most tasty leafy greens, plus it's incredibly good for you—full of iron, vitamin A, and antioxidants. Mixing it with cheese makes it doubly tasty. Use a prepared pastry case rather than making your own and it's doubly easy, too.

Serves 4

8-inch deep tart pan, lined with shortcrust pastry or a ready-made pastry case
10½ ounces spinach
3½ tablespoons butter
1 onion, finely chopped
2¼ cups Cheddar cheese, grated
2 medium eggs
2 medium egg yolks
¾ cup heavy cream
1 teaspoon French Dijon mustard
Salt and freshly ground black pepper

1. Preheat the oven to 400°F. Place the pastry crust in the oven and bake blind for 10 to 15 minutes.

2. Place a pan over medium heat and gently cook the spinach with half the butter until wilted. Remove from the pan and coarsely chop. Heat the remaining butter and fry the onions until soft. Line the bottom of the pastry crust with the spinach and onion.

3. Whisk together the cheese, eggs, egg yolks, cream, mustard, and seasoning. Pour over the spinach and onion and bake in the oven for 20 to 30 minutes, until the top is golden. Turn off the heat and let rest in the oven for 5 minutes before serving.

GREEN DREAM CLEANING MACHINE
*VEGETARIAN *DAIRY-FREE *GLUTEN-FREE

This juice is full of chlorophyll and rich in antioxidants, so important for cleansing and fighting damaging free radicals, but also very filling and nutritious. Swiss chard leaves contain at least 13 different antioxidants, plus a flavonoid called syringic acid, which has been shown to inhibit the activity of an enzyme that breaks down simple sugars, making this vegetable a great support for blood sugar control, very important when you are trying to control weight. Just look at these ingredients! You can't help but enjoy drinking this super-slimming green genie (pictured overleaf).

Serves 1

1 carrot
$\frac{1}{5}$ cucumber
A small bunch of parsley
A small handful of spinach
A small handful of Swiss chard
1 celery stalk
1 lime

Juice all the ingredients, mix together, and serve immediately.

Double up the quantities if you're serving to more than one person, but always make the juice fresh to get the most out of your ingredients.

WATERCRESS WONDER

*VEGETARIAN *DAIRY FREE *GLUTEN FREE

Watercress is a fantastic ingredient for juicing, not only for its great flavor, but because it's rich in many vitamins—A (in the form of beta-carotene), C, E, and K—and excellent in aiding calcium intake. Juiced with sulphur-rich asparagus, tart green apples, pineapple, and cucumber, it makes a light, fresh, tangy juice. The bromelain contained in pineapple assists in digestion by helping to break down proteins, making this deliciously healthy as well. You can also serve this juice as a yummy appetizer.

Serves 1

A large handful of watercress
4 asparagus spears
1 green apple
¾-inch thick slice of fresh
   pineapple, skin removed
¼ cucumber

Juice all the ingredients, mix well, and serve immediately.

Juicing is a fantastic way to extract nutrients from fresh fruits and vegetables, along with the water content, to produce a nutritionally rich and concentrated drink.

WARM CHICKEN
& WATERCRESS

*DAIRY-FREE *GLUTEN-FREE

Pink grapefruit is an underused ingredient but its interesting sweet/sour flavor works well with chicken. The marinated red onion is key and makes this a really memorable dish with great flavor and texture.

Serves 2 as a main course or 4 as an appetizer

1 large red onion, very
   thinly sliced
⅔ cup white wine vinegar
½ cup granulated sugar
2 Little Gem lettuces
1½ cups watercress
1 tablespoon olive oil
7 ounces cooked chicken,
   coarsely shredded
1 pink grapefruit, peel
   and pith removed, cut
   into segments

For the dressing
2 tablespoons extra
   virgin olive oil
2 teaspoons white wine
   vinegar
1 heaping teaspoon
   grainy mustard
1 teaspoon honey

1. Place the sliced red onion in a small heatproof bowl. Put the white wine vinegar and sugar in a small pan and heat gently, stirring occasionally, until the sugar dissolves. Increase the heat and bring to a boil. Pour the sweetened vinegar over the onions and leave to marinate for 10 minutes to 1 hour.

2. Separate the lettuce leaves and place in a large bowl with the watercress. Combine the dressing ingredients in a screw-top jar, shake well, then pour over the leaves. Toss well to combine.

3. Then, in a nonstick pan, heat a tablespoon of olive oil until very hot. Add the shredded chicken meat to the pan, leave for 2 minutes until starting to crisp up, then turn once or twice until it is golden and crispy.

4. On a serving dish, arrange the dressed leaves, grapefruit segments, and crispy chicken and top with the drained marinated onions.

This salad would be a good way to use up leftover Thanksgiving turkey instead of chicken.

LEEK, WATERCRESS & CHEESE VICHYSOISSE

This is one of the best chilled soups. The cheese adds a little tanginess which blends well with the leek and peppery watercress.

Serves 4

1 onion, chopped
3 leeks, chopped
3 tablespoons unsalted butter
1½ cups new potatoes,
   chopped
4 cups vegetable or
   chicken stock
3½-ounce bunch of watercress
5 tablespoons half-and-half
⅓ cup milk
3 ounces Roquefort cheese,
   crumbled
Salt and freshly ground
   black pepper

1. Sweat the onion and leeks in the butter for about 5 minutes, until beginning to wilt. Add the potatoes and cook for another 5 minutes.

2. Add the stock and bring to a boil, then reduce the heat to a simmer and cook for 25 minutes, until all the vegetables are soft.

3. Remove from the heat. Add the leaves from the bunch of watercress and let infuse in the pan for 5 minutes. Transfer to a blender and pulse to a smooth puree.

4. Put the half-and-half, milk, and Roquefort in a small pan and heat gently, stirring until smooth. Add to the soup, stir well, and season to taste. Pour through a fine strainer, then chill until ready to serve.

WATERCRESS & SALMON SALAD

*GLUTEN-FREE *DAIRY-FREE

Combining salmon with the peppery taste of watercress makes a very tasty and satisfying meal. Fresh or canned salmon can be used as both are rich in long-chain omega-3 fats.

Serves 2

For the dressing
3 tablespoons olive oil
1 tablespoon lemon juice
1 teaspoon mustard
1 tablespoon chopped
   fresh dill
1 teaspoon honey

1½ to 2 cups baby new
   potatoes (2 to 3 per person)
2 small stalks broccoli
   (about 3 ounces)
1¾ cups watercress, washed
   and dried
2 cooked salmon fillets,
   flaked, or 7 ounces canned
   salmon

1. Whisk together all the dressing ingredients until well combined and set aside.

2. Boil the baby potatoes for about 10 minutes or until just cooked, adding the broccoli for the last 1 to 2 minutes (you want it just tender, not overcooked). Drain and when cool enough to handle, slice the potatoes and chop the broccoli.

3. To assemble, place the watercress in a serving dish, add the salmon, potatoes, and broccoli, and drizzle with the dressing.

Use asparagus, when in season, to complement the broccoli.

SALMON RAVIOLI & WATERCRESS PESTO

The smoky flavors of the salmon, the creaminess of the goat cheese, and the peppery pesto make a delicious combination, and using the Fresh Dulse Pasta on page 52 to create the ravioli takes this dish to the next level. You can substitute flat-leaf parsley for the the watercress, if you prefer.

Serves 6

1 quantity Fresh Dulse
   Pasta (see overleaf)
5½ ounces soft goat cheese
5½ ounces smoked salmon,
   cut into pieces
Sea salt and freshly
   ground black pepper

For the watercress pesto
3½ ounces (about 3 cups)
   fresh watercress
⅔ cup extra virgin olive oil
3 tablespoons pine nuts,
   toasted
2 garlic cloves, peeled
½ cup Parmesan cheese,
   grated

1. Cut the dulse pasta into strips about 4 inches wide and place teaspoonfuls of goat cheese at 3-inch intervals down the strip. Season the smoked salmon with salt and pepper and place a teaspoon of it on top of each piece of cheese.

2. Fold the pasta over the filling and press down around it to seal it in. Cut out the pasta parcels with a sharp knife and crimp the edges with a fork to ensure that the filling doesn't ooze out during cooking.

3. Put a large saucepan of salted water over high heat and bring to a boil. Drop in the ravioli and cook for 5 minutes.

4. While the pasta is cooking, make the watercress pesto: Put the watercress, oil, pine nuts, garlic, and grated cheese in a food processor and blend for a couple of minutes.

5. Drain the ravioli from the water and return it to the saucepan. Pour the watercress pesto on top and toss gently.

6. Season with pepper and serve.

FRESH DULSE PASTA *VEGETARIAN *DAIRY-FREE

Ireland has an abundance of fantastic seaweed and over the past ten years it has started to make its way back on to menus across the country. Dulse, also known as dillisk, is a red algae that holds a subtle flavor of the sea and marries well with fresh pasta.

Makes approx. 2¼ pounds

4 cups whole wheat flour,
   plus extra for dusting
¼ cup dried dulse flakes,
   finely chopped
Large pinch of sea salt
7 large eggs
Semolina flour, for dusting

1. Place the flour, dulse, salt, and eggs in a food processor and blend together until a dough forms. Place the dough on a floured board and knead until smooth. Separate the dough into 6 balls, cover with a kitchen towel, and let rest in a cool place or in the fridge for 30 minutes.

2. If you have a pasta machine, set it up and push the dough through the rollers 8 times. With each pass through the rollers, reduce the setting, until you reach the final setting. Be careful that the pasta does not break as you should now have

a long, thin sheet. If you don't have a pasta maker, roll the dough out very thinly with a rolling pin. (This can be hard as it breaks easily—it's well worth buying a pasta maker as they are inexpensive and so useful.)

3. Then, dust the pasta sheet lightly with semolina flour and hang over a clean clothes horse or similar for 10 minutes. Store in the fridge, and eat within 2 days.

CAESAR SALAD *VEGETARIAN

This book could not be complete without this classic lettuce salad. The Romaine lettuce is packed with vitamin A, but the olive oil, used on the croutons and in the dressing, is also very nutritious. It contains healthy fats and antioxidants, so it is well worth purchasing premium-quality oil.

Serves 2

½ small ciabatta, cut
  into large cubes
Olive oil
Salt and freshly ground
  black pepper
1 extra-large egg
1 garlic clove, crushed
1 tablespoon lime juice
1 teaspoon vegetarian
  Worcestershire sauce
1 teaspoon Dijon mustard
1 Romaine heart, torn or
  roughly chopped
¼ cup vegetarian Parmesan,
  coarsely grated

1. Preheat the oven to 375°F. To make the croutons, toss the ciabatta in 1½ tablespoons of oil and season well. Spread on a baking sheet and cook until crisp and golden, about 10 minutes.

2. Place the egg in a pan, cover with cold water and bring to a boil. Boil for 1 minute, then transfer the egg to a bowl of cold water to stop it from cooking. Once it is cool enough to handle, crack the egg into a food processor and add the garlic, lime juice, Worcestershire sauce, mustard, and remaining oil. Process well, then season with salt and freshly ground black pepper to taste.

3. To serve place the lettuce in a serving bowl, pour over the dressing, and top with the croutons and Parmesan. Toss well and serve immediately.

GRILLED SARDINES & MACHE

*GLUTEN-FREE *DAIRY-FREE

This simple salad defies seasons—it makes a fitting lunch on a hot summer's afternoon, a nice appetizer for a winter festive meal, or a nutrient-packed anytime dish. Serve it family-style from a large platter or as individual servings on pretty plates.

Serves 4

1 medium fennel bulb, including stems and fronds
8 fresh sardines, cleaned, leaving head and tail intact
2 lemons
3 tablespoons extra virgin olive oil, plus more for brushing
½ teaspoon Aleppo pepper or pinch cayenne
Fine sea salt and freshly ground black pepper
4 ounces mache or lamb's lettuce

1. Finely chop half the fennel, including half the fronds.

2. Rinse the sardines and pat dry, then spread out on a platter. Finely zest 1 lemon over the top, turning the sardines to cover both sides. Drizzle with ½ tablespoon of the oil and sprinkle the outside and cavities with the fennel stems, Aleppo pepper, and a generous ¼ teaspoon of salt.

3. Squeeze 2 teaspoons of lemon juice into a small bowl and set aside. Cut the remaining whole lemon crosswise into ⅛-inch thick rounds. Discard the seeds.

4. Heat an outdoor grill or a grill pan until hot. Brush with oil and grill the sardines, in batches if needed, for 4 to 5 minutes per batch, turning once until just cooked through. Using a metal spatula, transfer the cooked fish to a large, clean plate.

5. Lightly season the lemon slices with salt and black pepper, then grill for about 1 minute on each side until lightly charred. Transfer to a large bowl.

6. Thinly shave the remaining half fennel bulb and place in the bowl with the lemon. Add the reserved lemon juice, the remaining 2½ tablespoons of oil, half the fennel fronds, ½ teaspoon salt, and a generous pinch of black pepper; toss to combine. Add the mache and very gently toss to combine.

7. Divide the salad and the sardines between four serving plates and garnish with the remaining fennel fronds.

If cooking on a grill, use a grill pan to prevent the lemon slices from slipping into the coals. If you can't find mache, any small tender lettuce will do.

FATTOUSH SALAD WITH RADISH

*VEGETARIAN *DAIRY-FREE

Fattoush is an eastern bread salad made with toasted pita and fresh vegetables. Once all the vegetables have been sliced it's very quick to put together—perfect for a relaxed summer lunch. Plus it's bolstered by vitamins A and K from the Little Gem lettuces, to help protect and heal skin.

Serves 4

1 cucumber, peeled, seeded, and cut into ½-inch dice
3 pita breads
2 cloves garlic, minced
Juice of 1 lemon
3 tablespoons extra virgin olive oil
2 Little Gem lettuces, coarsely shredded
6 radishes, sliced
1 red onion, finely chopped
5 ripe tomatoes, peeled, seeded, and coarsely chopped
4 tablespoons coarsely chopped purslane leaves
2 tablespoons each coarsely chopped flatleaf parsley, cilantro leaves and mint
Salt and freshly ground black pepper

1. Place the diced cucumber in a colander, sprinkle with salt, and let drain for 20 minutes.

2. Meanwhile, toast the pita bread, then cut into small strips

3. In a large bowl, mix together the garlic, lemon juice, and olive oil to make a dressing.

4. Wipe off any excess salt from the cucumber and add to the bowl along with the diced vegetables, herbs, and pita and toss well to coat with the dressing. Season with salt and pepper and serve immediately.

ARUGULA, RASPBERRY & GORGONZOLA

They serve something similar to this salad in the beautiful Olympic café in Kalk Bay, which sells some of the best coffee in South Africa. They don't bother with the usual formal café rules, and operate as a hodge-podge of rustic charm and enviable style.

Serves 4

2 tablespoons olive oil
2 big chunks of brown
  bread, cut into croutons
½ teaspoon salt
1¾ cups raspberries, the
  plumpest you can find
3 ounces wild arugula
  (about 3½ cups)
5½ ounces Gorgonzola,
  pulled into chunks

For the dressing
2 tablespoons raspberry
  vinegar
1 teaspoon Dijon mustard
2 tablespoons extra virgin
  olive oil

1. You need to make the croutons first so they aren't too hot when they hit the salad leaves: Heat the oil in a medium frying pan and when the oil is sparking a little, add the bread. While the croutons are in the pan, throw in a little salt and cook until they all have a crunch. Keep tossing the pan so one side doesn't brown more than the other.

2. To make the dressing, put all the ingredients in a glass measuring cup or bowl and mix as thoroughly as you can—try do this without splashing the dressing and staining your shirt!

3. Combine the raspberries, arugula, and Gorgonzola in a bowl and pour over the dressing. Toss together (gently so you don't bruise any of those arugula leaves) and add the croutons. Serve in a big pile on an even bigger plate.

Try to find raspberry vinegar for the dressing—it's a valuable ingredient to have in your pantry—but if you find it hard to come by, use white wine vinegar instead. If you're a vegetarian, use a vegetarian alternative to gorgonzola, such as dolcelatte.

BUTTERNUT SQUASH & ARUGULA SALAD

*VEGETARIAN *GLUTEN-FREE *DAIRY-FREE

This is a great low-carb lunch and is Paleo-friendly. Butternut squash is the perfect vegetable replacement to satisfy all your carb cravings.

Serves 4

1 large butternut squash, peeled and halved (seeds discarded)
2 tablespoons olive oil
1 tablespoon chopped thyme
1 tablespoon honey
8 ounces arugula leaves
¾ cup toasted pumpkin seeds
Freshly ground black pepper

For the dressing
¼ cup olive oil
Juice of ½ lemon
Juice of ½ orange
1 teaspoon Dijon mustard
1 teaspoon chopped thyme leaves

1. Preheat the oven to 425°F.

2. Chop the butternut squash into wedges and place in a large bowl. Drizzle with the oil, add the thyme, and toss to coat. Place on a baking sheet and cook in the oven for 30 minutes. Every 10 minutes, remove the baking sheet and toss the squash so that all the edges become roasted and caramelized.

3. After 30 minutes, toss one last time, drizzle with the honey, cook for another 5 minutes, then set aside to cool slightly.

4. Meanwhile, mix all the dressing ingredients together and dress the arugula leaves in a large bowl. Scatter the pumpkin seeds on top and toss with the butternut squash. Finish with a few grinds of black pepper and serve.

Butternut squash has a lovely sweet, nutty taste so you don't have to do much to it. It's lovely raw, but it's really perfect roasted, when it caramelizes beautifully.

SWISS CHARD, ALLSPICE & POMEGRANATE

*VEGETARIAN *DAIRY-FREE *GLUTEN-FREE

Like so many cabbages, Swiss chard greets spices and fruits like old friends—they get along very well together, and any potential austerity is further softened by a mass of golden fried onions and a generous addition of cilantro.

Serves 6

3 tablespoons extra
   virgin olive oil
2 large onions, peeled, halved,
   and finely sliced across
A good tablespoon of vinegar,
   (white wine or cider)
1¼ pounds Swiss chard
½ teaspoon allspice
Sea salt
1½ cups cilantro leaves,
   coarsely chopped
Sumac (optional)
3 heaping tablespoons
   pomegranate seeds

1. Heat 2 tablespoons of oil in a large saucepan over medium heat and cook the onions for 15 to 20 minutes, stirring frequently, until creamy and golden.

2. At the same time bring a large saucepan of water to a boil and acidulate it with the vinegar. Cut the chard leaves off the stalks and thickly slice them, then thinly slice the stalks. Add the stalks to the pan and cook for 5 minutes, then add the leaves and cook for another 2 minutes. Drain in a colander and shake dry.

3. Stir the allspice into the onions, and then add the chard. Season with salt and gently cook for a couple of minutes to acquaint the ingredients, then stir in the cilantro. Transfer to a serving dish, drizzle with the remaining tablespoon of oil, scatter with some sumac if wished, and then the pomegranate seeds. Serve at once.

BRASSICAS

KALE CHIPS
*VEGETARIAN *GLUTEN-FREE *DAIRY-FREE

Kale is all over the place—on restaurant menus, at farmers' markets, on supermarket shelves—and kale chips are the snack of the moment. It's super nutritious—curly kale works best for this recipe.

Makes lots

9 ounces curly kale
2 tablespoons extra
   virgin olive oil
Sea salt
Sugar

1. Preheat the oven to 300°F. Strip the leaves off the kale, tear into bite-sized pieces, and put in a bowl. Sprinkle with extra virgin olive oil, a little salt, and a pinch of sugar, and toss well. Spread out in a single layer on two baking sheets.

2. Bake in the preheated oven for approximately 20 minutes until crisp. Transfer to a wire rack to cool and crisp further. Enjoy.

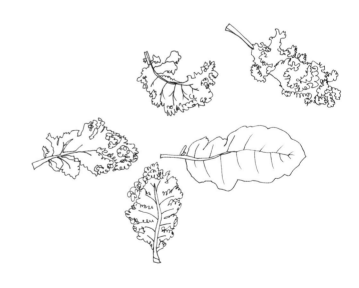

WILD RICE, KALE & POMEGRANATE

*VEGETARIAN *GLUTEN-FREE *DAIRY-FREE

This hearty salad is a very modern recipe that is packed with superfoods and classic Turkish ingredients. The combination of the mixed rice—using black, red, brown, and white—gives the salad a variety of colors, textures, and flavors. Turkish staples dill, parsley, mint, pomegranate seeds, and walnuts add flavor, and the addition of kale gives it a light, modern twist. The dressing uses sumac to give an extra sour note. A little pinch of this ground red berry is a lovely way to introduce more depth of flavor to any salad dressing.

Serves 4 to 6

1¾ cups mix of black, red, brown, and white rice
5½ ounces kale
A handful of finely chopped dill
2 handfuls of finely chopped flat-leaf parsley leaves
A handful of finely chopped mint leaves
1 red chile, seeded and finely chopped
1¼ cups pomegranate seeds
½ cup walnuts, lightly crushed

For the dressing
¼ cup olive oil
3 tablespoons pomegranate molasses
Juice of 1 lemon
1 teaspoon superfine sugar
1 teaspoon of sumac
Sea salt and freshly ground black pepper

1. Cook the rice in a large pan of boiling water according to package instructions, starting with the variety that takes the longest and adding the rest at appropriate times so that they all cook perfectly. Drain and rinse under cold running water. Set aside to drain.

2. Meanwhile, cook the kale for 2 to 3 minutes in a large pan of boiling water. Drain and refresh under cold running water. When cool, drain thoroughly and squeeze out the excess water with your hands.

3. Whisk all the dressing ingredients together in a small bowl.

4. Put the drained rice in a large mixing bowl and add the kale, herbs, chile, and half the pomegranate seeds and walnuts. Pour in three-quarters of the dressing and mix everything together thoroughly.

5. Transfer the salad to a serving dish and pour over the remaining dressing. Top with the remaining pomegranate seeds and walnuts and serve immediately.

SPROUTING GREENS JUICE
*VEGETARIAN *DAIRY-FREE *GLUTEN-FREE

This is a seriously green juice—in color and taste. If you choose only one skin-saving juice—make it this one! Kale is a true skin superfood, not only rich in Vitamin K, but also highly prized among nutritionists for its omega-3 content and over 40 different flavonoids that make it both an antioxidant and anti-inflammatory. Broccoli sprouts have been shown to contain levels of sulforaphane 100 times higher than those found in the plant itself. Sulforaphane is a compound that improves the liver's ability to detoxify, an essential process for skin clarity and overall health.

Serves 4

4 to 5 handfuls of kale
A handful of parsley
2 kiwi fruit, peeled
1 lime
A handful of broccoli
  sprouts
½ teaspoon spirulina

Juice all the fruit, vegetables, and sprouts, and then stir in the spirulina before serving.

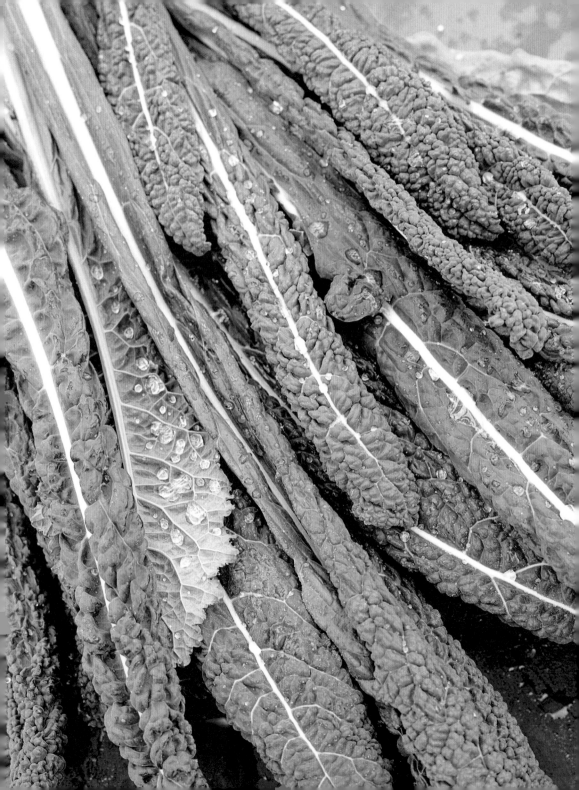

PAPPARDELLE WITH CAVOLO NERO *VEGETARIAN

Cavolo nero—kale's Italian cousin, also known as black kale—is a nutrition powerhouse, and combining it with heart-healthy garlic makes this dish extra good for you. You can swap the crème fraîche for yogurt for an extra health-boost, but watch the sauce carefully as it can easily split.

Serves 4

7 ounces pappardelle
2 tablespoons olive oil
4 garlic cloves, finely
   chopped
7 ounces cavolo nero, stalks
   removed, coarsely chopped
Salt and freshly ground
   black pepper
⅔ cup white wine
4 tablespoons crème fraîche
4 tablespoons freshly
   grated vegetarian
   Parmesan, plus extra
   to serve

1. Bring a large saucepan of salted water to a boil. Add the pappardelle and cook for 6 to 8 minutes, until *al dente*.

2. Meanwhile, heat the olive oil in a medium saucepan, then add the chopped garlic. Add the cavolo nero and stir to wilt in the oil. Season with salt and pepper. Add the white wine and boil for 3 to 5 minutes until reduced.

3. Stir in the crème fraîche and Parmesan. Drain the pasta, mix into the sauce, and serve immediately with some extra Parmesan sprinkled on top.

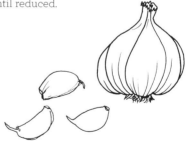

CAVOLO NERO WITH SOBA NOODLES *VEGETARIAN *DAIRY-FR

Delicate and beautiful, these noodles are tossed with a sweet ginger dressing and pepped with lime. There is plenty of blanched cavolo nero and bright avocado for good measure. You can eat this with extra soy sauce for a salty edge.

Serves 4

9 ounces soba noodles
1 head of cavolo nero
   (about 7 ounces)
1 ripe avocado
4 scallions, sliced
¼ cup sesame seeds,
   to garnish

For the dressing
1 to 2 garlic cloves, crushed
1 teaspoon tamarind paste
1½-inch piece of fresh ginger,
   peeled and finely grated
1 tablespoon maple syrup
2 tablespoons extra virgin
   olive oil
2 teaspoons sesame oil
finely grated zest and juice
   of 1 organic lime

1. Cook the soba noodles by adding them to boiling water and simmering according to package instructions, usually for about 5 minutes. Drain and rinse well under running water until cool.

2. Meanwhile, separate the cavolo nero leaves and then trim the tough base of each. Coarsely chop them and cook in a pan of lightly salted boiling water for 3 to 4 minutes, until tender. Cool and drain well, then squeeze out any excess water and coarsely chop.

3. Make the dressing by putting all the ingredients (including any ginger juice) into a jar and mix well until combined.

4. Cut the avocado flesh into ¾-inch chunks and set aside.

5. Put the noodles and cavolo nero into a large bowl and pour over the dressing. Combine thoroughly before carefully mixing through the avocado and scallions; a light touch will mean the avocado doesn't turn to mush.

6. Serve on plates sprinkled with sesame seeds.

BRAISED CAVOLO NERO *VEGETARIAN

Crinkled black kale is known as cavolo nero (black Tuscan cabbage). Serve it on its own, as a vegetable or as a topping for polenta.

Serves 4 to 6

4 heads cavolo nero
Sea salt and freshly
   ground black pepper
3 tablespoons extra
   virgin olive oil
2 garlic cloves, peeled
   and finely sliced
Extra virgin olive oil
Bruchetta, toasted

1. Remove the stems from the cavolo nero leaves. Blanch in a large pot of boiling, well-salted water for 3 to 5 minutes. Be careful not to overcook. Drain well.

2. Heat the olive oil in a heavy-bottomed saucepan. Add the garlic and cook gently. When it begins to color, add the cavolo nero and season generously with salt and pepper.

3. Cook for about 5 minutes. Transfer to a bowl and drizzle generously with extra virgin olive oil.

4. Serve on top of broiled or toasted bruschetta.

QUINOA CABBAGE ROLLS

Try varying this recipe by adding some nuts, or serve the quinoa as a dish on its own sprinkled with Gruyère. Try substituting the cabbage with chard leaves.

Serves 4

½ ounce dried porcini
  mushrooms
4 tablespoons olive oil
1 onion, finely chopped
2 stalks celery, finely chopped
2 carrots, finely chopped
3 garlic cloves, finely chopped
1½ cups white mushrooms,
  finely sliced
½ cup quinoa
¾ cup red wine
Sea salt and freshly
  ground black pepper
½ cup cooked chickpeas
1 large cabbage, such as
  Savoy
2 (14-ounce) cans crushed
  tomatoes
1 teaspoon sugar
Pinch of sea salt
3½ ounces grated Gruyère

1. Preheat the oven to 350°F.

2. Cover the porcini with 1¼ cups of boiling water and let soak. Meanwhile, heat half the oil in a medium-sized saucepan. Add half of the onion, celery, carrots, and garlic and cook over medium heat until softened. Add the white mushrooms and cook for another 3 minutes.

3. Add the quinoa and cook for a minute, stirring all the time. Pour in the soaked porcini and their liquid, add half the wine, and season generously. Bring to a boil, reduce the heat to a simmer, cover, and cook for approximately 15 to 20 minutes until tender and most of the liquid has been absorbed. Once cooked, season as necessary and stir in the chickpeas.

4. Bring a large pan of salted water to a boil. Using a small knife, carefully remove the core from the cabbage, peel away 8 to 12 leaves, and cook in the boiling water for 5 minutes or until softened. Drain and run under cold water to refresh, then drain again.

5. Remove the tough center stalks and lay the leaves on a work surface, vein side down. Place approximately 2 heaping tablespoons of quinoa mix on one half of the leaf and roll up, folding the sides in to form a package. The size of the leaves will differ, so fill and wrap accordingly. Place in a large ovenproof dish, seam side down.

6. Heat the remaining oil over medium heat, add the remaining onion, celery, carrots, and garlic, and cook until softened. Add the remaining wine and tomatoes, sugar, and salt and bring to a boil. Reduce the heat and simmer until reduced by half. Pour over the cabbage leaves, cover with foil, and cook in the oven until tender, approximately 40 minutes.

7. Serve hot, sprinkled with Gruyère cheese.

CABBAGE & HONEY SALMON *DAIRY-FREE *GLUTEN-FREE

Honey and ginger are two of the best ingredients—they create magic when cooked together. Both are also excellent for the immune system, so this makes a lovely dinner all through the winter months.

Serves 4

4 × 10½-ounce skinless salmon fillets

For the glaze
2 tablespoons honey
1 tablespoon Dijon mustard
Juice of 1 lemon
1-inch piece of fresh ginger, peeled and grated

For the cabbage
3 tablespoons olive oil
1 small cabbage, sliced into thin strips
1 garlic clove, crushed
1 tablespoon sesame seeds, plus extra to garnish
Freshly ground black pepper
4 scallions, chopped

1. Heat a large, nonstick pan over high heat and add the salmon—if you have a good-quality, nonstick pan, there should be enough oils in the salmon to cook it without the need to add any extra. Cook the salmon for 3 to 4 minutes on each side.

2. Meanwhile, make the glaze: Place the honey, mustard, lemon, and ginger together in a bowl and stir to combine. Set aside.

3. When your salmon is just about cooked, spoon the glaze over the top, then take off the heat. The glaze will caramelize in the hot pan and turn the salmon sticky and brown.

4. To cook the cabbage, heat half the olive oil in a wok over medium heat. Add the cabbage and stir-fry for 3 to 4 minutes, then add the remaining oil and cook for another 5 minutes, tossing all the time (if you need more moisture, add a drop or two of water). Add the garlic and sesame seeds and cook for another minute.

5. Turn the cabbage onto a plate, season with black pepper, and top with the glazed salmon. Scatter the scallions over the top and serve with a few extra sesame seeds.

WOK-FRIED CHOI SUM WITH SHIITAKE

*DAIRY-FREE

Asian-style greens are much more commonplace than they used to be, thanks to the growth of interest in Thai and Chinese cooking. All the ingredients for this dish are readily available—so get to wok!

Serves 4

1 pound choy sum
2 tablespoons peanut oil
1 garlic clove, crushed
1 tablespoon finely
   chopped fresh ginger
1½ cups shiitake mushrooms
½ cup (about 3 ounces)
   fresh or canned Chinese
   water chestnuts, peeled
   and thinly sliced
⅓ cup chicken stock
2 tablespoons cornstarch
2 tablespoons tamari
1 tablespoon sesame oil
1 tablespoon roasted peanuts

1. Separate the stems from the leaves of the choy sum and cut them into 2-inch long pieces. Blanch the stems in boiling salted water until just tender, then drain well.

2. Heat a wok or deep frying pan, add the peanut oil, garlic, ginger, choy sum stems, mushrooms, and water chestnuts and stir-fry for 3 to 4 minutes. Add the choy sum leaves and cook for a minute longer.

3. Blend the stock with the cornstarch to form a paste and stir it into the pan. Stir in the tamari and sesame oil and toss well. The sauce should form a glaze around the vegetables. Sprinkle with the peanuts and serve immediately.

PORK ROAST WITH BROCCOLI RABE

*GLUTEN-FREE

Pork and seafood is a great combination as their flavors augment each other. Here, they are used in a dish straddling the French/Chinese cuisine line. Young green garlic and *gai lan*, or Chinese broccoli, are stewed in butter and finished with tender bay scallops. Fermented black beans add a subtle umami layer that ties the dish together. The combination of flavors is like a symphony. It is stunning.

Serves 4

⅓ cup fermented black beans
Pinch of ground cloves
Pinch of ground cardamom
1 teaspoon ground coriander
1 tablespoon chopped
   young garlic, plus
   ⅓ cup thinly sliced
2 pounds pork loin
Sea salt and freshly ground
   black pepper
2 small stalks gai lan
   or broccoli rabe (about
   9 ounces)
1 tablespoon julienned
   fresh ginger
4 tablespoons unsalted
   butter, softened
8 ounces bay scallops, rinsed
Rice wine vinegar

1. In a small pot over high heat, combine ½ cup water with the black beans, spices, and chopped garlic. Boil until reduced by three-quarters. Transfer to a blender and puree until smooth. Set aside.

2. Season the pork with salt and pepper. In a large frying pan over high heat, sauté the pork loin, fat side down, until browned and crisp, or about 7 minutes.

3. Drain the rendered fat from the pan and save for another use. Turn the pork over and cook until browned, or about 10 minutes more.

4. Reduce the temperature to low and cook until the interior of the loin is cooked but still rosy, or about 5 minutes more. Transfer to a clean platter to rest for 10 minutes.

5. Return the frying pan with the pan drippings to the heat and add the gai lan, sliced garlic, and ginger. Cook until the gai lan begins to wilt, then add the butter and cook for 1 minute more.

6. Remove the pan from the heat and add the scallops. Season with salt and vinegar. The scallops will warm through as the pan cools.

7. Thinly slice the pork and divide between four dinner plates. Top with the black bean puree and garnish with the gai lan mixture. Serve immediately.

STIR-FRY WITH SPRING VEGGIES *VEGETARIAN

Crisp fresh fava beans and broccoli are good sources of fiber—pair them with bok choy and you have a quick and delicious meal providing vitamins A and C as well as potassium.

Serves 4

7 ounces noodles of your choice
1 tablespoon vegetable oil
2 cups purple sprouting or broccolini, cut into small florets
4 garlic cloves, finely chopped
½-inch piece of fresh ginger, finely chopped
1 red chile, seeded and finely sliced
A bunch of scallions, sliced
1 cup fava beans, cooked and peeled of outer skins if large
2 heads bok choy, thickly sliced
1½ tablespoons hoisin sauce
1 tablespoon soy sauce (add extra to suit your own taste)

1. Bring a large saucepan of water to a boil and cook the noodles according to the package instructions, or until just tender. Drain well and rinse with cold water to stop them cooking more.

2. Heat the oil in a nonstick wok or frying pan. Add the broccoli, then cook over high heat for 5 minutes or until just tender, adding a little water if it begins to stick. Add the garlic, ginger, and chile, cook for another minute, then toss in the scallions, fava beans, and bok choy. Stir-fry for 2 to 3 minutes.

3. Add the hoisin and soy sauces and warm through. Toss the noodles in with the vegetables to warm and serve.

ROASTED BROCCOLI
WITH BULGUR *VEGETARIAN

Broccoli should be given more attention. Florets are so often forced to sit on the side of a plate, lacking luster and boiled beyond recognition, but this should not be their destiny. With careful cooking and a few sophisticated ingredients—tart dried cherries, bulgur wheat, and pistachios—the broccoli steps up and tastes unrecognizably chic.

Serves 3

1 healthy sized head of
  broccoli, divided
  into florets
2 tablespoons olive oil
1 cup bulgur wheat
Sea salt and freshly
  ground black pepper
¼ cup dried cherries,
  plus a few to garnish
½ cup pistachios,
  coarsely chopped
Zest of 1 organic lemon

For the dressing
3 tablespoons Greek yogurt
2 tablespoons red wine
  vinegar
1 tablespoon extra virgin
  olive oil

1. Preheat the oven to 350°F. Spread the broccoli florets out on a pan and drizzle them well with olive oil. Put them in the oven to roast for 20 minutes.

2. Meanwhile, make your bulgur wheat by pouring it into a large bowl and seasoning. Pour in ⅔ cup boiling water. Cover the bowl with plastic wrap and allow it to sit for 10 minutes. Remove the plastic wrap, fluff the bulgur wheat up with a fork, and stir in the dried cherries, pistachios, lemon zest, and roasted broccoli.

3. To make the dressing, mix all the dressing ingredients together with a dash of hot water. Pour the dressing over the salad and gently toss until well combined. Serve in one, two, or three bowls garnished with a few extra dried cherries. Serve immediately.

BRUSSELS SPROUTS WITH PARMESAN

Brussels sprouts cooked in boiling water and tossed with butter are enjoyable enough, but rather uninspiring. This recipe is a more interesting way to prepare them, combining tiny Brussels with sweet onions and a dusting of fresh Parmesan.

Serves 4 as a side

3 tablespoons olive oil
20 small pearl onions, blanched and peeled
1 tablespoon light brown sugar
3 tablespoons unsalted butter
¾ cup beef stock
¾ cup baby Brussels sprouts
2 tablespoons freshly grated Parmesan cheese
Salt and freshly ground black pepper

1. Heat the oil in a frying pan large enough to fit the onions in a single layer, add the onions, and cook over high heat until golden all over. Add the sugar and half the butter and cook until the onions are caramelized, about 8 to 10 minutes. Pour in the stock and cook until it has evaporated.

2. Meanwhile, cook the Brussels sprouts in boiling salted water until just tender but still retaining a little bite. Drain them well.

3. In a separate pan, heat the remaining butter until foaming, add the sprouts, and sauté for 5 minutes, until golden. Add the onions and toss together, then season with salt and pepper and transfer to a serving dish. Sprinkle with the Parmesan and toss to coat.

Brussels sprouts are a strange vegetable, inspiring either love or hate. Here are some great ways to serve them:
• Tossed with the roasted chestnuts and celery
• Pureed and finished simply with nutmeg and butter
• Mixed with cream and seasoned with a little curry powder

SHAVED BRUSSELS
SPROUTS *GLUTEN-FREE

Very thinly sliced raw Brussels sprouts tossed with lots of good-quality extra virgin olive oil, zingy lemon juice, and peppery, slightly tart aged sheep cheese is enough to convert even the most ardent sprout-adverse folk. Try it when Brussels sprouts are in season, from late August to March, and see for yourself. This salad loses its lemony punch if it sits for too long, so serve immediately.

Serves 4 to 6

1 pound Brussels sprouts
5 tablespoons good-quality
  extra virgin olive oil
½ teaspoon fine sea salt
3½ tablespoons fresh
  lemon juice
½ teaspoon whole black
  peppercorns, crushed
4 ounces semi-soft pecorino
  cheese studded with
  black peppercorns,
  very thinly shaved

1. Rinse the Brussels sprouts, then pat dry with paper towels. Remove any outer leaves that have brown spots or have yellowed, then cut the sprouts in half, lengthwise. Very thinly slice the sprouts crosswise, transferring the sliced pieces to a large shallow serving bowl as you go. Discard the stems.

2. Drizzle the oil over the sprouts, then sprinkle with the salt and toss well to combine. Add the lemon juice, then the crushed pepper, and toss once more. Lay the cheese over the top of the salad and serve immediately.

In speciality cheese shops and delicatessens, you may find semi-soft pecorino cheese studded with black peppercorns; it will often be labeled rustico. If you can't find one with peppercorns, add more crushed peppercorns to this dish.

INDEX

ACKNOWLEDGMENTS

The publishers would like to thank the following for kind permission to reproduce their recipes:

Eric Skokan © pp12, 84 from *Farm Fork Food*

Rachel DeThample © pp15, 16 from *Less Meat More Veg*

Paul Gayler © pp19, 27 from *Pure Vegetarian*; pp23, 47, 83, 91 from *Passion for Veg*

Jimmy Garcia © p20 from *Social Eats*

Margaret Rayman © pp24, 44, 49 from *Healthy Eating to Reduce the Risk of Dementia*

Mindy Fox © pp28, 34–35, 54, 93 from *Salads: Beyond the Bowl*

Annie Rigg © p30 from *Summer Berries & Autumn Fruit*

Darina Allen © pp33, 67 from *30 Years at Ballymaloe*; p77 from *Forgotten Skills of Cooking*

Annie Bell © pp38, 62 from *Low Carb Revolution*

Liz Earle © pp41, 43, 71 from *Juice*

Clodagh McKenna © pp50–52 from *Clodagh's Irish Kitchen*

Georgina Fuggle © pp58, 74, 88 from *Take One Veg*

Dan Green © pp61, 80 from *The Paleo Diet*

John Gregory-Smith © p68 from *Turkish Delights*

Maria Elia © p79 from *The Modern Vegetarian*

Published in 2016 by Kyle Books
www.kylebooks.com

Distributed by National Book Network
4501 Forbes Blvd, Suite 200,
Lanham, MD 20706
Phone: (800) 462-6420
Fax: (800) 338-4550
customercare@nbnbooks.com

10 9 8 7 6 5 4 3 2 1

ISBN 978-1-909487-56-7

Text © see page 95
Design © 2016 Kyle Books
Illustrations © 2016 Jenni Desmond
Photographs © see below

Pages 2, 22, 29, 34–35, 55, 93 © Ellen
Silverman; 4 (left), 8, 32, 66 © Laura
Edwards; 4 (right), 25, 45, 48 © Will Heap;
5 (left), 31, 51, 52 © Tara Fisher; 5 (middle
and right), 6–7, 13, 56, 85 © Con Poulos;
10–11, 21, 36–37, 60, 64–65, 81 © Clare
Winfield; 14, 17, 72, 76, 86 © Peter Cassidy;
18, 26, 82, 90 © Gus Filgate; 39, 63 © Dan
Jones; 42, 70 © Georgia Glynn-Smith;
46 © Steve Lee; 59, 75, 89 © Tori Hancock;
69 © Martin Poole; 78 © Eva Kolenko.

Cover photographs: top row, left to right
© Will Heap; Laura Edwards; Will Heap;
Tori Hancock; second row, left to right
© Tara Fisher; Georgia Glynn-Smith;
Tori Hancock; Con Poulos.

Project Editor: Claire Rogers
Designer: Helen Bratby
Illustrator: Jenni Desmond
Production: Nic Jones and Gemma John

Library of Congress control No.:
2016939831

Color reproduction by ALTA London
Printed and bound in China by C&C Offset
Printing Co., Ltd.

* Note: all eggs are free-range